RIDING THE RIVER

Congregational Outreach
And the Currents of the 21st Century

Paul Mundey

ANDREW
CENTER
RESOURCES

RIDING THE RIVER
Congregational Outreach and the Currents of the 21st Century

Paul Mundey

This book is based, in part, on concepts originally presented in an article in *Brethren Life and Thought*, Volume XXXVI, Summer, 1991, Number Three.

Biblical quotations, unless otherwise noted, are from the New Revised Standard Version of the Bible, copyrighted 1989 by the Division of Christian Education, National Council of Churches, and are used by permission.

ISBN 0-9637206-1-9

Manufactured in the United States of America

CONTENTS

When you pass through the

      waters, I will be with you;

And through the rivers, they

      shall not overwhelm you.

          Isaiah 43:2a

RIDING THE RIVER

Congregational Outreach
And the Currents of the 21st Century

Paul Mundey

Introduction

All of us carry a certain number of ambitions and desires which we've not yet fulfilled but have hopes of accomplishing in the future. I look forward to the day I go white water rafting for the first time. The possibilities of navigating a wild and risky river spark the very heart of who I am. Perhaps that's why I'm basically hopeful for the future. Though the river of time looks foreboding and the currents swift, there is also the promise of creative struggle, surprising challenge, and true adventure.

The church has traditionally been cautious in navigating the river of time. We are inclined to fear where the tides of tomorrow may take us. Resisting the currents, we have tended to cling to the riverbank, which seems safe, secure, and predictable.

That tendency, while understandable, has no doubt contributed to the decline which many churches have experienced. The bank of the river is not necessarily a safe place, for strong currents can cause significant erosion. Many people, especially the young, are not attracted to timid bands, huddling on supposedly safe ground - people are drawn to groups that are going somewhere, navigating rather than avoiding the currents before them.

There are several persons who have attempted to chart the waters which are before us and who have helpful counsel for those of us eager to leave the bank and enter fully into God's tomorrow. This report deals with the opportunities and concerns which are suggested by these futurists, researchers, and prophets. We'll look together at key trends and currents which are before us, affecting congregational outreach and growth; and then I'll draw some conclusions concerning the best ways to "ride the river."

The "Flow" of the Future

Without exception, futurists predict that the remainder of the twentieth century and the start of the twenty-first century will be times of unprecedented change. Writers consistently maintain that the "flow of the future" will be swift, marked by marvelous innovation. Indeed the rate of change itself is expected to keep increasing, so that each year brings more changes than the one before.

Some researchers understandably worry about the possibility that the rate of change will be too great for people. In 1970, futurist Alvin Toffler wrote a book, the title of which expresses what many feel today: *Future Shock*. Under the pressure of an increasingly rapid rate of change, Toffler accurately predicted that some people would feel overwhelmed and would long for "stability zones," which were not characterized by the same rate of change as the rest of society. The desire for those stability zones is no doubt one of the reasons some congregational leaders have resisted change in the life of the church. As already suggested, however, the refusal to change can cause other problems, because the banks by the rapidly moving river of time are not as safe as they may appear.

Some analysts have even suggested the possibility that there should be a base rate of change, like a desired rate of interest, inflation, or unemployment. While such an approach would be desirable in many ways, it would be very difficult to slow the rate of change across such diverse fields as government, industry, construction, and nonprofit organizations, including the church.

The world of business and technology has been pressing hardest on the throttle of change. Technological innovations in recent years have been clever, indeed mind-boggling. "Smart houses" are already becoming a reality and include technology which turns light on and off as one enters a room, adjusts the thermostat based on the person in the room, automatically activates a security system under certain circumstances, and lets one's voice activate television and stereo systems. Laptop computers already can handle tasks which required a room full of computer equipment only a few years ago, cellular phones and FAX machines have become commonplace, and the pace of medical innovation is astounding. The fascination of the United

States, Canada, and many other nations with "gizmos and gadgets" will increase rapidly along with technological sophistication.

Naming the Currents

The pace of change in business and technology will also be reflected in other areas of life. A number of significant demographic and lifestyle changes are already having impact on all forms of ministry, especially that of the local church. Consider the following areas:

• **Baby Boomer Dominance**. The 12:01 AM January 1, 1946 birth of Kathleen Casey in a Philadelphia hospital signaled the beginning of an unprecedented BOOM in the birth of children for the United States. From then until 1964, an estimated 75,875,000 babies were born in the United States. Over two million more boomer-aged persons migrated to the United States, bringing the boomer total at the start of the nineteen-nineties to around 78,000,000. Close to a third of all Americans now living were born between 1946 and 1964. Thus we should not be surprised that baby boomer values dominate so much of American culture. All indicators suggest that this trend will continue into the future, multiplying in importance as boomers eventually reach the retirement years.

Because of their numbers, boomers have been the subject of considerable study and analysis. Many observers have pointed out that boomers seem especially hooked on self-fulfillment. That changes their view of employment, leisure time, parenting, marriage, civic organizations, and the church. They are much more likely than earlier generations to ask the question: "What's in it for me?" When moving from one community to another, they don't show the same kind of denominational loyalty which most of their parents did. It's normal for them to "church shop," evaluating the programs and benefits of different churches against their own criteria of what they need from congregational membership. Some boomers have rejected the church entirely.

Tex Sample, in *U.S. Lifestyles and Mainline Religion*, suggests that boomers place great importance on the value of life and do not feel that life should be denied. That view has made many of them strongly identify with the peace movement and be critical of military expansion. The issue of abortion, however, remains a difficult one for boomers. While they are more likely than their parents to support freedom of choice, they are by no means of a single mind on this issue.

Many boomers also believe that life is to be creatively and emotionally expressed - that is to say that life should be lived in full disclosure. Boomers are not as likely as their parents to hold back observations and comments out of the fear of offending someone else. This makes it relatively easy to know their thoughts and feelings about various issues, but can also be disconcerting to older persons who are more cautious about expressing their opinions.

Boomers also represent a psychology of affluence. As children and teenagers, they did not have to endure some of the deprivations which came to earlier generations. The economy has continued to expand during their lives, making them aware of the opportunities for profitability and not often reminding them of the losses which some people must endure in order for others to gain. Boomers see self-fulfillment as a life-long process and as an important goal for all people.

The boomer self-fulfillment ethic expresses itself in a variety of ways. For example, the divorce rate for the baby boomer generation is five times the rate for their parents' generation. Fifty-two percent of all boomers are divorced by the age of the age of thirty-four. Many will marry again, but some will have to search long and hard for a new mate.

Boomers also tend to be reluctant to make long-term commitments. They would rather not join organizations which require open-ended, drawn out obligations. This is another reality that has made some uncomfortable with church member-ship, which represents a major commitment.

Boomers also have intense interest in products and services which reflect exceptional quality. They are the first generation to have grown up with television. By age eighteen, the average baby boomer has spent over 24,000 hours watching television. This has made boomers accustomed to "switching channels" (having a variety of options) and to expecting the very best performance from others.

The population bulge of the baby boomers will not disappear when the first one gains gray hair. By the year 2025, Americans over the age of sixty-five will outnumber teenagers by more than two to one. According to the Census Bureau, by 2030 the median age is expected to have reached forty-one. Some claim that the median age will eventually reach fifty.

Because of their numbers and their focus on self-fulfillment, boomers will continue to cause stress and change wherever they go. They also have the necessary energy to accomplish great things.

• **Women in the Lead.** During the nineteen seventies and eighties, women gained a growing prominence in the American work force. Women will in fact be in the lead in the nineteen nineties and beyond. John Naisbitt and Patricia Aburdene point out in *Megatrends 2000* that the days of women as a work force minority have ended: "In business and many professions, women have increased from a low of 10% in 1970 to a critical mass ranging from thirty to fifty percent in much of the business world" (Naisbitt and Aburdene, p. 217). The circulation of *Working Woman* magazine has grown from 450,000 in 1981 to over 900,000 today - surpassing *Forbes, Fortune,* and finally *Business Week.*

Women will not only be present in greater numbers; they'll also be in more positions of influence. For many years, American business was dominated by a macho, military management style. Heavy-handed, sometimes coercive strategies were utilized to mobilize an organization. The trend today, however, is away from control-oriented management to vision-oriented leadership. Values such as shared power, participatory decision-making, and customer satisfaction as a top priority mark this approach.

Many business communities are waking up to the leadership gifts of women. When one moves out of the military model, men and women are equally capable of motivating people toward high quality work.

As women continue to become a vital part of the work force, day care and elder care benefits (related to the parents of aging baby boomers) will need to expand and increase.

A significant decline in volunteerism is also part of this shift. Women at one time constituted the majority of volunteers for community service, social organizations, church work, and school activities. This is no longer the case. Women are increasingly employed outside of the home during the day and then are swamped with traditional household responsibilities in the evening. This means that they are not available for volunteer work at the same level which was taken for granted in the past. Many people have interpreted the decline in volunteerism as a loss of commitment to the church, which is not necessarily the case.

• **Ethnic Expansion.** During the late nineteen eighties and the early nineteen nineties, America accepted huge numbers of immigrants relative to most other countries. Between 1980 and 1990, the total population of the United States increased about ten percent. The native-born population of the country only grew by four percent during that period of time. As the following chart shows, the Hispanic population increased at five times the rate of the native-born population, and the Asian population increased at twelve times the native-born rate. During the rest of the nineties, the percentage of the population which consists of African Americans, Hispanics, and Asians will continue to grow. By the year 2010, minorities will account for a third of our population.

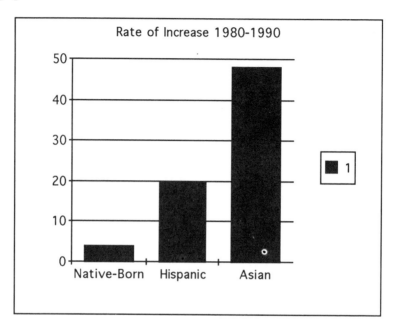

This multicultural influence will multiply across the United States during the twenty-first century, and this will especially be the case in urban areas. The traditional "melting pot" theory of ethnic assimilation will not hold true. Most ethnic groups have little interest in blending into white, Anglo culture. There will be more movement toward clear preservation of one's own heritage, along with an involvement with American culture as a whole.

The Rodney King incident in Los Angeles and the resulting riots, courtroom struggles, and media focus made us painfully aware that we have not yet learned how to live peacefully and justly with those of other ethnic backgrounds. Disproportionate numbers of blacks, Hispanics, and Native Americans populate the jail and prison cells of our country; and that is a growing source of resentment among minority people. The perception of increasing numbers of minority persons is that the opportunities which are available to white people are not necessarily as readily available to other races.

The future, then, demands that we learn to live with ethnic expansion and enhancement, not ethnic conformity and "meltdown." As America becomes more and more multicultural, it will become important to recognize *and celebrate* the treasure of our diversity. We must find ways to help persons of all races find the opportunities which they need for meaningful life.

• ***Shifts in Population.*** Closely related to ethnic expansion is the shift in population centers across the United States. Urban areas, especially in the South and Southwest, will continue to experience growth. The 1990 census showed that California's growth, in and of itself, was larger than the total population of many states. Consider the difference in rates of growth among the different regions between 1980 and 1990:

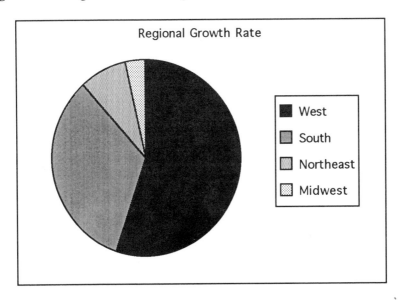

All ten of the areas projected to add the most to their population between now and the year 2000 are in the southern or western parts of the country:

Los Angeles	Anaheim
Dallas	Atlanta
Oakland	Tampa
St. Petersburg	Phoenix
San Jose	Denver

The fastest growing states in the coming decade will be Arizona, New Mexico, Florida, Georgia, Alaska, Hawaii, New Hampshire, and California.

No change in the relatively high rate of mobility for the United States is anticipated. While aging baby boomers may long for more permanence, a rising divorce rate, economic transitions, and the boomer self-fulfillment ethic will tempt a significant percentage of the population to look for greener pastures.

• **A Passion for Play.** Americans love to play. In response to a *Rolling Stone* magazine survey, the vast majority of people said that, if given an extra hour in the day, they would use it for leisure or recreational activities. George Barna, in his book *The Frog in the Kettle*, predicts that: "During the coming decade, the value of leisure time will heighten because people will find less and less fulfillment from their jobs, their marriages, and their existing social networks."

The longing for play may also be contributing to a general devaluing of work. Some decline in the work ethic seems to be a sign of the times. With tardiness increasing, sick leave abuse up, and quality control down in some fields, it appears that job security and high pay are not the motivators they once were.

• **Economic Boom.** The decline in work ethic, however, does not appear likely to slow the economy. While there are many economic concerns, it remains true that a ready flow of goods, services, and money appears available as we move into the twenty-first century. We are moving from a national economy to a true global economy.

With trade restrictions having loosened and more open relationships with some countries being in place, the economy is truly more and more a global one. John Naisbitt and Patricia Aburdene raise interesting questions in *Megatrends 2000*: "U.S. companies create and sell $81 billion in goods and services in Japan. Is that part of the U.S. economy or the Japanese economy? Are Korean stocks purchased in London by a Turk part of the Korean, British, or Turkish economy?" [p.19].

Beyond this general impetus for global economic boom, there are also a variety of other catalytic factors, pointing toward prosperity. Naisbitt and Aburdene include in that list: "the powerful drive of telecommunications, the relative abundance of natural resources, competition for reduced taxes, greater concern about world peace, and a more major focus on the environment" [p.31].

In a 1990 book called *Powershift*, Alvin Toffler speaks of those and other changes being responsible for the creation of a "super-symbolic economy." He sees the entire power structure of the planet going through radical change if not outright disintegration from what we have known in the past. "A key unnoticed reason for this global shake-up is the rise of a radically new system for wealth creation in which information (including everything from scientific research to advertising hype) plays a dominant role. This new system for making wealth is totally dependent on the instant communication and dissemination of data, symbols and symbolism. It is a super-symbolic economy" [p.86]

These rapid changes in work, lifestyle, habits, and the economy create great opportunities for some, but will cause major problems for others. Toffler warns that these changes produce "cleavages that fanatics rush to fill. It arms all those dangerous minorities who live for a crisis in the hopes of catapulting themselves onto the national or global stage and transporting us all into a new Dark Age" [p.92].

It's not a pretty picture - but it is the other side of booming, rapidly changing economics.

• **The Plight of the Poor and Powerless.** Indeed the rapidly changing economic situation places ever increasing levels of stress on those who are on the bottom side of the economy and of the changing power structure. As many jobs are made obsolete, the new ones which are created tend to be in three categories: those which involve significant technical, communication, or organizational skill; those which are at or barely above minimum wage (such as fast food and order fulfillment jobs); and those which are part-time or temporary rather than full-time or permanent. In 1992 two-thirds of all new jobs created were temporary - meaning that those persons had no security and no benefits.

Persons who have limited levels of education are increasingly at a disadvantage in the job market. This reality also adds to the racial tension discussed earlier in this booklet because so many of those on the bottom of the educational and economic systems are of minority races. In *Two Nations: Black and White, Separate, Hostile, Unequal*, Andrew Hacker points out that there is currently almost a 200 point gap between black and white scores on SAT tests [p.141]. That gap has very real economic ramifications. In 1992 the ratio of unemployed black workers to unemployed white workers was 276 to 100 [*The New York Review*, April 23, 1992]; preliminary figures for 1993 show an even greater disparity. While many people are becoming millionaires as a result of the economic transitions in the world, that success does not fall equally. In the last ten years, only three black people have been among the 791 listed by *Forbes* magazine as the richest in the United States.

Andrew Hacker also shares the disturbing reality that "a man living in New York's Harlem is less likely to reach sixty-five than is a resident of Bangladesh" [p.45-46]. Obviously we want to see improved life expectancies for all people, including those in places like Bangladesh; but it is particularly disturbing to realize that a country like the United States continues to have so many serious discrepancies in the quality of life for its citizens.

The problem of violence in the United States has increased significantly, and it is especially disturbing to note the numbers of children and young people who are both the victims and the perpetrators of violent acts. While violence in the media and the too easy availability of weapons certainly contribute to an environment which feels unsafe, the root causes of poverty and powerlessness will have to be addressed before our streets are made significantly safer. Crime becomes a too attractive option for those who are not competing successfully in a difficult job market, and weapons become a cheap source of power for those who feel themselves powerless.

While the comparisons between black and white Americans are especially striking, depressing statistics could also be shared for other ethnic minority groups, including Hispanics and Native Americans. Comparative statistics aside, however, the realities of hunger and homelessness strike far too many people; and many futurists fear that the years ahead will bring increasing disparity between the rich and the poor. This stands as a dark cloud over some of the more promising aspects of the future.

• **Denominational Decline.** Though there is some difference of opinion, most forecasters predict the continued decline of denominations. The current erosion of denominations, especially the so-called "mainline" ones, is well documented. The Presbyterian Church (USA), the United Methodist Church, and the Episcopal Church are among those who have been hard hit.

There are numerous reasons for the continuing decline of denominations. One of the most prominent is the wave of individualism sweeping American culture. As mentioned in the baby boomer discussion, many persons no longer affiliate with an organization primarily because of heritage, tradition, or blind loyalty. This reality has been true of baby boomers and seems even more true of generations which have come after them. Today many Americans and Canadians "shop" for a church just as they comparison shop at the grocery store. This trend toward consumerism not only means new challenges for churches seeking to reach newcomers to the neighborhood or community but also means there are no guarantees of keeping present members. Poor sermons, dirty restrooms, inattentive childcare, or bad music may prompt those already in a church to look for alternatives.

We've also experienced a significant blurring of boundaries among various ecclesiastical groups. It's increasingly difficult to tell the difference between a Methodist and a Presbyterian, for example. While some of the distinctions among the mainline Protestant denominations in the past have no doubt been artificial, we now experience a diminished awareness and appreciation of the distinctive heritage of mainline churches. Without that awareness and appreciation, there's no reason for people to maintain denominational loyalty.

Other factors in the decline of membership in mainline denominations include the increasing mobility of people which removes many from their "roots" (including hometown churches); the increased number of parachurch organizations, some of which are self-identified as nondenominational, and which have offered high quality programs; and the attitudes toward church membership of baby boomers and the generations after them. In *It's a Different World*, prominent church consultant Lyle Schaller identifies an even greater source of decline as "the blatant failure of many groups to reach out and evangelize" [p.72]. Churches in the mainline denominations have simply not been sufficiently aggressive in reaching out to gain new members to replace those lost by death and relocation.

While it is too early to predict whether denominational decline will equal denominational demise, the trends are cause for concern. Mainline churches must move away from too much dependency on traditional denominational styles and methods which do not offer promise for the future. All churches will be challenged in the years ahead to increasingly find ways to change and reach out more effectively.

• *Religious Revival.* Ironically, even as futurists are predicting denominational decline, they are also anticipating religious revival. These two seemingly contradictory forecasts reveal much about the spiritual longings of present and future generations. Though persons increasingly disdain staid, institutional religious forms, there is, nevertheless, a yearning for intimacy with the transcendent.

In Gallup polls since 1988, over 59% of the respondents have shared the conviction that their churches or synagogues are too concerned with "organizational as opposed to theological or spiritual issues." The same polls show that vast numbers of people believe in God without being convinced that the institutional church is a place where their faith can be nurtured.

Consider, for example, how people continue to respond to polls and surveys about their relationships with God and with religious institutions:

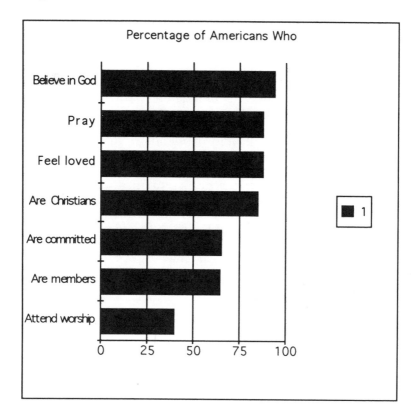

The vast majority believe in God, pray, and feel loved by God. Most identify themselves as Christians. Far smaller percentages identify themselves as deeply committed, actually belong to a church, or attend worship on a regular basis.

When churches offer ministry which is perceived as spiritually alive, people, including baby boomers, do respond. The Riverbend Baptist Church in Austin, Texas is one interesting example of this reality. Boomers are showing up there in record numbers. The church downplays traditional, institutional demands and emphasizes instead what might be called a "common sense religion" that connects individual needs with the Christian message. Typical sermon titles at that church include:

16

"Winning Is Beginning"; "Wait to Worry"; and "There's a Yes in Every Mess."

Established Protestant congregations are not the only groups attempting to connect with the spiritual longings of boomers and the generations following them. Scores of other religious movements are on the rise. Gordon Melton, the editor of *The Encyclopedia of American Religions*, has estimated that 400 new spiritual groups came into existence just between 1987 and 1989.

The New Age movement is one example of these spiritual causes and apparently appeals to between five and ten percent of the population. Traditional religion has been perceived by many as a matter of the soul, whereas New Age thinking includes a holistic emphasis on body, mind, spirit, the environment, and even business. It also includes far greater focus on the individual's intuition. One can effectively argue that the Jewish and Christian faiths, properly understood, are holistic in nature; but that is not the perception of many who are unchurched.

It appears likely to many futurists that the United States will increasingly become more pluralistic in religious identification and affiliation and definitely less Protestant. Many, like Harvey Cox, feel that the contemporary shape of religion is "a global phenomenon that has to do with the unraveling of modernity," or the faith that science could master all problems. Others link spiritual resurgence with the traditional religious image of the millennium - the turn of the century.

The Catholic Church has likewise experienced many changes in the last three decades, with increasing numbers of persons unwilling to accept its official teachings and practices. Yet persons raised in the Catholic Church retain concern about spiritual matters even while resisting the authoritarianism which their parents and grandparents more readily accepted. Catholic theologian Matthew Fox has written widely about the spiritual life, making connections with ancient Catholic writings like those of Meister Eckhart, Hildegard of Bingen, and Julian of Norwich, and linking Catholic thought with that of Protestantism, Judaism, and even the New Age perspective. While occasionally an embarrassment to Rome, he's won a wide following, influencing a great many young priests and keeping some Catholics in the fold.

Novelist and priest Andrew Greeley regularly produces fiction which would be expected to make a nun or priest blush, but he has a continuing concern about the spiritual life and about what the Catholic Church can be at its best. Like Fox, he has a large following and considerable influence, perhaps not always positive from the standpoint of Christian orthodoxy, but an inspiration, nevertheless, to many who would otherwise have given up on the church as an organization. Both Fox and Greeley have also had considerable influence on many Protestants and agnostics.

Whereas enlightenment thinkers (and even some theologians of that time) predicted the disappearance of religion in the twentieth century, just the opposite seems to have occurred in the United States. While denominations may struggle to retain influence and numbers in the decades ahead, there is considerable evidence that spiritual matters will increase in their importance to the public as a whole.

Navigating Tomorrow

How do we successfully travel the currents just described, especially in the quest for church revitalization and growth which has become a necessity for so many denominations and local churches? What follows are some practical suggestions for navigating the future.

1. Focus on being a missionary leader. With Protestantism moving to what may well be minority status, the image of living in a foreign land comes to mind. Simply acquiescing to the dominant values around us will no longer be an option. Increasingly we will be called to challenge and engage the belief systems of others.

Kennon Callahan identifies this kind of ministry stance as the mark of the *missionary pastor or leader.* Such a person does not passively wait for the church to form, renew, or grow on its own; rather, he or she "makes it happen" through active, concerted outreach.

There was a time when ministry styles focused around the image of the "professional minister." Church growth strategies concentrated on providing quality programs and services and on outreach to those who visited the various services or groups of the church. While the issue of quality will take on even greater importance in the years ahead (as discussed in suggestion six below), just offering quality programs and responding to those who visit will not be enough in a culture with diverse approaches to meeting spiritual needs and with little respect for denominational loyalty. There won't be enough visitors to replace those who move and die from the congregation over a period of time.

Visitors come to church increasingly because of the initiative of the pastor and of church members. Church leaders must learn how to positively interpret the Christian message, while still showing respect for those who approach spiritual matters from other perspectives. Opportunities to share the faith must be sought throughout the community, and that faith must be directly related to the needs of those outside of the church. In earlier decades, authors like C.S. Lewis were sometimes referred to as "apologists," because they interpreted and defended Christianity to a readership which was often not familiar with Christian beliefs or teachings. Missionary leaders must see themselves as apologists, interpreting the message of the church in intentional, relational ways to a public which may have little real knowledge of the Christian faith.

As important as quality programs and visitor follow-up will

remain, far more initiative must be taken to get people to visit church in the first place. The pastor must learn how to reach out in those ways and must learn how to train members of the church in missionary skills.

2. Learn to "thrive on chaos." Even a cursory glance toward the future suggests that "the way ahead" will be marked by turbulence; the status quo will be disturbed and a general sense of unsettledness and restlessness will emerge. In his book *Thriving on Chaos*, Tom Peters argues that a healthy response to such "revolution" is not to bemoan it or to run from it. Rather our calling as leaders is to accept the chaos as a given and learn to thrive on it. The chaos can, in fact, become a source of advantage and opportunity rather than a problem. What a hopeful word for those engaged in congregational outreach, growth, and revitalization; opportunity is born out of adversity (a common lot for mission-minded people)!

The unsettledness and restlessness will without a doubt cause people to be searching for meaning, purpose, and stability. While the church cannot afford to remain unchanging in the midst of such a swiftly moving culture, the age-old messages of love, grace, forgiveness, and acceptance may well find increasingly receptive audiences. The ministry of the church should positively reach out to those whose lives are in turmoil.

3. Go to where the people are. The United States population is moving to the cities and to the South/Southwest, and so must the church - especially as we speak of new church development. This will require several changes on our part, including a new willingness to encounter and include ethnic people. There is no way we can go to the cities and to the South and ignore the mushrooming populations of Koreans and Hispanics - to name two ethnic groups in particular.

As George Barna has observed, "The Church in America has promulgated Christianity as a white man's faith for many decades. If the Church hopes to stem its current decline in numbers and influence, it must embrace minorities not only as equals, but as a key to future impact in ministry" [p.193]. Going to where the people are will mean embracing some people we are not accustomed to embracing - thus expanding the parameters of our witness and of the church.

Reaching out to minorities in the name of Christ also means taking seriously the social inequities which make life difficult for many ethnic groups. The church must be concerned about those who are poor and powerless, about those who are left behind by the rapid changes which make some people wealthy.

We may find that some new churches should be started in storefronts and by pastors who may be part-time at first, earning their living at another trade. Most mainline denominations need to make significant adjustments in order to gain more clergy of minority races.

4. Target your outreach to specific audiences. As we have discovered, baby boomers will not commonly "show up" in church because of brand loyalty; their self-fulfillment ethic calls them - rightly or wrongly - to different criteria for participation. At the top of their list of criteria is the question: *Does it (a particular church or ministry) meet my needs?*

The implications of this reality are major. We can no longer simply put up a church building, open the doors, and expect people to come. A new strategy is in order, whereby we *connect life within the church to the real needs of people outside the church.*

Since it is impossible to be all things to all people (though many congregations try), the way ahead requires us to "target" specific audiences, to identify their needs, and to deploy specific ministries in their direction. Only the largest of churches can truly offer ministries to meet the needs of many diverse audiences. Most churches will find that a focus on single persons, on young families, on particular ethnic groups, on persons concerned about pressing social issues, or on persons in need of various support groups will yield better results than trying, with limited personnel, space, and budget, to be all things to all people.

5. Utilize contemporary methods and means. Tomorrow's trends are filled with the unpredictable and the exciting; yet, for the most part, the church continues to be marked by the predictable and the unexciting. **The number one indictment against the church continues to be: it's boring!**

Congregations of the future - both existing and new - must begin adopting contemporary methodology. This may include such things as:

- Placing synthesizers and drums alongside organs and pianos.
- Utilizing drama and video alongside choirs and sermons.
- Using computer technology to maintain accurate records and provide mailings and publicity which are indeed more, rather than less, personal.

In addition, new consideration needs to be given to church architecture and to the times for weekly services. Who said that stained glass windows and steeples were church building requirements? What's wrong with the presence of a large viewing screen in the sanctuary? Why can't there be chairs rather than pews and altar furnishings which can't be moved? Does church school have to be on Sunday? Why can't worship be on Friday or Saturday evening rather than Sunday morning?

It's easy for us as Christians to become too concerned that changes in *form* will result in content being lost. By refusal to modify forms, however, we may be guaranteeing that the content will never be heard by large numbers of people. In *Christianity in Culture,* Charles Kraft wrote: "The dynamic of Christianity... is not in the sacredness of cultural forms... [but] in the venture-someness of participating with God in the transformation of contemporary cultural forms to serve more adequately as vehicles for God's interactions with human beings" [p. 318].

The matter of changing forms, however, is one which generates considerable controversy in many churches because of the threat those changes represent to persons wanting to see the church as a stability zone. It's important for all members of the church to be helped to distinguish between form and content and also to recognize the necessity of more effectively reaching out to those outside the church. In many instances churches will find that they can handle some of these differences by increasing options. Rather than making radical changes in the ten o'clock Sunday morning service of worship, for example, it may be possible to offer a more innovative service at eleven on Sunday morning or at five, six, or seven on Friday or Saturday evening.

6. Become ruthless about quality. Another characteristic of boomers, as already discussed, is their insistence on quality - high quality. Being the consumers that they are, there is little tolerance for mediocre ministry from the church. This requires a radical rethinking of church life and formation.

While the image of the "professional minister" referred to in the first suggestion includes concern about quality, that concern has generally not gone far enough. The church has too often been a place for "leftovers" - leftover furniture and equipment, leftover time and energy, and leftover creativity. Tomorrow's church will need to be characterized by the very best.

This requirement does not need to translate into elegance or showcasing. It does, however, require a new attention to detail (in such matters as church property, for example) and a new level of excellence in all aspects of the church's program. Think about the message communicated by the level of quality your church currently offers in:

- The music at worship services.
- The sermon.
- Church school classes.
- Youth groups.
- The childcare offered during worship and other church activities.
- The restrooms.
- Parking.
- The church newsletter.
- Signs marking the way to the church.
- The external appearance of the church.

It takes the kind of missionary style described in the first suggestion to get people to visit the church for worship, classes, or other activities. It takes consistently high quality to *keep* them coming!

7. Downplay the institutional side of religion. As one thinks again of baby boomers and the generations following them plus the decline in denominationalism, this directive comes as no surprise. The trends show little empathy for an emphasis on "organized religion." Savvy congregations, then, will view themselves as institutionally linked, but not institutionally bound. There's a big difference.

Institutionally bound congregations relate to their parent denomination in a codependent fashion. Rather than taking the vision of the parent body and making it their own, institutionally bound churches simply parrot the party line.

Institutionally *linked* congregations will be accountable to their denominations but not dependent on them. They will "think for themselves," making faith and tradition come alive in an indigenous and contemporary fashion. By operating in this way, their main identity will not be a particular "label on the lawn," but new life in Christ as it takes root in their own particular locale.

This also means changes for denominational agencies. Rather than seeing local churches primarily as a base of support for regional and national level programs and ministries, the agencies need to see their role as encompassing the support and nurture of the local church, recognizing the importance of customizing services to individual situations. Local churches which receive positive, responsive service from denominational agencies are generally more than willing to support those ministries which can best be performed beyond the level of the local church.

8. Emphasize the "main thing." As Herb Miller points

out in *The Vital Congregation*, "Every human endeavor has a 'main thing.' Putting out fires is the main thing for fire fighters. They do other things like fire prevention education, but a lack of effectiveness at their main thing spells... failure" [p. 28]. While churches do a variety of things, their **main thing is to help people meet their spiritual needs and deepen their faith in God in meaningful ways.**

Given the spiritual hunger of our time, certain failure awaits us in our church development efforts if we neglect our *main thing*. People approach both new and existing congregations for one principal reason: to find God. Unless they meet people who know God (not just *about* God) and shed light on God's reality and fullness found in Jesus Christ, they will continue their search elsewhere.

9. Help people learn how to live. As the trends indicate, the years ahead will not only be changing times, but times of upheaval. Violence, divorce, and crippling stress will be on the increase. Some people will be scrambling just to stay alive. Global and systemic issues are crucial to Christian faithfulness; however, unless we help folks sort out their everyday lives, they will have little energy for larger issues.

Our worship and education must become more relevant, addressing the pain and struggle of real life. In worship, we need to make use of music which is lively and praise-oriented (hymns to God, rather than about God); and our preaching should accent the pragmatic, boosting people into the work week with meaningful counsel on how to live effectively. In education, we need to give people opportunity to discuss the problems of daily life and to share with one another strategies which are successful in meeting and overcoming those problems. The message of the gospel needs to be brought into direct relationship to the needs of people.

10. Strive to form a deeper sense of community. Alvin Toffler predicts that future change and turbulence will overwhelm even the political structures of society. Undoubtedly this will spill over into other aspects of organizational and group life.

People are not only hungry for spiritual meaning and faith; they are also desperately in need of a sense of belonging, of community. The rapid changes in society will in fact deepen that need for almost everyone.

There is an urgent need, then, for the church to be the church. As traditional, organizational settings become saturated or collapse, the church will become a primary arena where people can connect and belong. Support ministries for the divorced, twelve-step groups, Bible study fellowships, potluck meals, and other opportunities will become more and more important as congregations live out the biblical vision of Christ's "new community."

11. Organize by the maxim "simple says it best." With the decline of volunteerism and a new valuing of leisure time, congregations need to organize in a leaner and simpler fashion. Expecting boomers, in particular, to get involved in a lot of bureaucratic duties, as well as active ministry, is unrealistic. There is simply not enough discretionary time in their lives.

In *The Cameo Church*, Rick Warren counsels that the contemporary, future-bound church will "operate without a lot of traditional committees, boards, and elections. With a simple structure, less time [will be] spent on maintaining the organization and more time... spent on actual ministry" [p. 164].

Many of our churches take enormous amounts of time to make decisions. It's not uncommon for a proposal for a new program to be introduced in a board meeting one month, referred to a committee of the board for discussion the next month, referred to finance for consideration the following month, be discussed again at a board meeting the next month, and then be put on the agenda for a congregational meeting two months later. Six months time can quickly pass, during which the need for the ministry or the enthusiasm of those who originally proposed the ministry may have disappeared.

Simpler decision-making structures in the church require that we reach greater levels of trust in one another and that we get past the need for a few people to tightly control everything that happens. High standards of quality can be maintained without requiring that every new idea go through a lengthy approval process.

This also means that church leadership needs to take a more open, accepting view of innovation. We need to learn not to unnecessarily block the ideas of other persons and not to needlessly throw roadblocks in the way of ministries about which others are enthusiastic. The model used by the Church of the Savior in Washington D.C. is an exciting one, because most of the work is done through "mission groups" which generate the volunteers and other resources necessary to conduct important ministries.

12. Keep the Christian experience both challenging and fun. As the economy booms and many Americans increasingly play, there is a growing need for congregations, both new and existing, to represent Christianity as lively and alert. In all candor, far too many churches are too stuffy and serious. In the jargon of pop psychology, they do a wonderful job of validating and admonishing the adult side of discipleship, but they do a lousy job of affirming the childlike side of discipleship.

We dare not downplay the costly aspects of Christianity; the times are too urgent for that. If we do not also represent the joy of our faith, however, we run the risk of appearing lifeless. Congregations eyeing the future, then, will loosen up; they will encourage laughter both in the parking lot and the sanctuary; they will value both serious reflection and a rousing good time.

Conclusion

In the film *The Dead Poets Society*, Robin Williams portrays a competent but revolutionary teacher. Employed by a very proper, private school, he soon finds himself at odds with the ethos of the place. In a culture of tradition, he encourages innovative thinking; in a climate of conformity, he invites students to trust their instincts.

As the film progresses, one is struck by the sense of vision characterizing Williams and his students. A sense of tomorrow is written across their faces as they begin to see - and live out - future possibilities. The underlying philosophy of such conviction is fuzzy at first, until Williams' motto sinks in: "Seize the day!" he counsels his students, "Seize the day!"

These are wise words for the rest of us as we, too, eye tomorrow. Facing future trends does not happen on the sidelines of life; rather the future is found as we seize the moment, as we seize the day - grasping possibilities that might just be. The image of "riding the river" is yet another way of saying the same thing. As we leave the bank, enter the flow, name the currents, and navigate the water, we somehow find and claim the future.

How the church needs to find and claim the future! As we continue to cling to what we have always known and been, the tides of tomorrow are working in reverse, tending to erode us, not energize us. There is an urgent need, then, for leadership to "take to the water," to wrestle with the currents, to embrace what is yet to be. Those who are most successful will plan carefully for the trip, learning as much as possible about the waters ahead.

New congregations, in particular, are called to be in the forefront of such initiative. With a fresh start, a clean slate, new churches are in a unique position to "try on" the future, to pour new wine into new wineskins, to demonstrate new paradigms for a new day, to dream new dreams, to see new visions for a new millennium.

C.S. Lewis once observed that Christians are far too willing to settle for far too little. "We are," he wrote, "like children playing in mud puddles, when we could be enjoying luxury cruises at sea." The currents of the twenty-first century will accommodate few luxury cruises but will welcome an unlimited number of risky rafters, persons game enough to chart wild waters, individuals bold enough to read uncertain winds and then move - move into God's adventurous future.

For Individual and Group Reflection

While you may be reading this report as an individual, the issues which are raised are also excellent for discussion by local church planning groups, boards, committees, task forces, and classes. The material works especially well when covered in three sessions, though the issues raised may produce discussion and change which will continue long after the formal study of the report has been completed.

If you are reflecting on this report as an individual, you'll find helpful ideas in the session outlines which follow. If you are working with a group or class, modify the ideas as appropriate for your setting.

Session One

Riding the River Reference: This is an initial session, so it is possible that group participants may not yet have received individual copies of the report. The only report sections to which specific references are made are the *Introduction* [p.5-6] and *The "Flow" of the Future* [p.6-7].

Optional Preparation: Videotape the opening minutes from an episode of a popular science fiction program like *Star Trek: The Next Generation, Deep Space Nine,* or *Babylon 5.*

1. If you were able to videotape the opening of a science fiction program, show that clip to the group. Point out to the group that science fiction deals with events which are presumably far in the future, but that the popularity of science fiction says much about how rapidly our world is changing.

If a videotape segment is not possible in your setting, then begin by sharing something which has made you aware of the fast rate of change in society. That could be an experience with a computer or another aspect of technology; something you've read in this report or elsewhere; or something that a child or young person has said or done.

Ask group members to begin listing some of the major changes they anticipate happening in the next ten years. These may be changes in technology, in economics, in social structures, or in other aspects of life. Record group input on newsprint.

2. For biblical perspective on the future, read (or have a volunteer read) **Exodus 3:1-12**. Discuss as a group:

• Why did Moses find it difficult to accept the

responsibility he was given?
- What fears would Moses have had about the experiences ahead of him?
- Why do some people respond to thoughts about the future with uneasiness and fear while others are filled with a sense of excitement and adventure?
- What can we learn from the experiences of Moses to help us as we look at the future?

3. Summarize in your own words the major ideas shared in the *Introduction* and in *The "Flow" of the Future* from **Riding the River**. Point out that the purposes of this session and of the two which follow are to look together at some of the major changes affecting our society and to better understand the implications of those changes for the life of the church.

4. Give each group member a sheet of paper and a pen or pencil. Have each person share the major changes which he or she hopes can take place in the coming ten years in his or her own life; in the world in which we live; and in the life of your local church.

Have people divide into pairs to share those changes with one another. Then talk about the changes as a group, recording hoped for changes in the church on newsprint.

5. Close with prayer, thanking God for the past, the present, and the future.

Session Two

Riding the River Reference: *Introduction* [p.5-6] and *Naming the Currents* [p. 7-18].
Optional Preparation: Provide a display of books about the future. This might include some of the titles listed as *References and Resources* at the end of this report.

1. Summarize briefly the "riding the river" concept as described in the *Introduction*. Point out that, while it is important for the church as a whole to "ride the river," people will be at different points in how they feel about that process. Go around the group, asking each person to share with which of these categories he or she most strongly identifies when it comes to "riding the river":
- Staying on the shore as long as possible
- Willing to ride the river but not happy about it
- Eager to ride the river

2. For biblical perspective, have group members focus on **Exodus 14:1-31** which describes the crossing of the Red Sea.

Although the story is familia·, the passage of Scripture is fairly long. You can give group members time to read the verses in silence, or have volunteers read the passage aloud. Then talk about these questions:

- How would you have felt if you had been Moses approaching the Red Sea? How does that compare to your feelings about the future of the church?
- What can we learn from the experience of Moses and the Israelites which increases our confidence in what the future will bring?

3. Have each group member rate from "1" (low importance) to "5" (high importance) the following currents as they relate to your local church and to the denomination of which you are a part:

Current	Local	Denomination
Baby Boomer Dominance	——	——
Women in the Lead	——	——
Ethnic Expansion	——	——
Shifts in Population	——	——
A Passion for Play	——	——
Economic Boom	——	——
The Plight of the Poor and Powerless		
Denominational Decline	——	——
Religious Revival	——	——

Record responses on newsprint so that you can determine the major issues which seem of importance to your local church.

4. Spend time talking as a group about the top three or four "currents" which seem of importance to your local church. What are the implications of those currents for the future? Are there differences between the currents which seem important to your local church and those which seem important to the denomination? If so, why?

5. If the books on display are available for loan, invite group members to check out titles in which they are especially interested. Then close with prayer, thanking God for the opportunities brought to the church by changes in society.

Session Three

Riding the River Reference: *Navigating Tomorrow* [p.19-26] and *Conclusion* [p.27].

1. Go around the group, asking each member to briefly share something positive or something negative about your local church as it would be viewed by someone who was not a

member. Record those on newsprint as they are shared. Talk about the responses:

- Why did we share primarily positive (or negative) things?
- Why is it difficult to see the church from the perspective of a nonmember?
- What changes for our church do our comments suggest are needed?

2. For a biblical perspective, look at **Luke 10:25-37**, the familiar story of the Good Samaritan. Tell the story in your own words, or have a volunteer read it aloud. Then discuss:

- What groups in today's society would be comparable to the Samaritans?
- What does the attitude of Jesus toward the injured man suggest about how we should relate to the unchurched?
- What does the attitude of Jesus toward the Samaritan suggest about how we should relate to the unchurched?

3. Have group members rank from "1" (low importance) to "5" (high importance) the following guidelines from *Navigating Tomorrow* relative to the needs of your church:

_____ 1. Focus on being a missionary leader.
_____ 2. Learn to "thrive on chaos."
_____ 3. Go to where the people are.
_____ 4. Target your outreach to specific audiences.
_____ 5. Utilize contemporary methods and means.
_____ 6. Become ruthless about quality.
_____ 7. Downplay the institutional side of religion.
_____ 8. Emphasize the "main thing."
_____ 9. Help people learn how to live.
_____ 10. Strive to form a deepened sense of community.
_____ 11. Organize by the maxim "simple says it best."
_____ 12. Keep the Christian experience both challenging and fun.

Record responses on newsprint so that you can determine the major issues which seem of importance in your local church.

4. Spend time talking as a group about the top three or four guidelines for your local church. What specific steps do you need to begin taking to implement those guidelines?

5. Close with prayer, giving thanks to God for the life of the church and seeking help in reaching those outside the church.

References and Resources

Barna, George, **The Frog in the Kettle** (Ventura: Regal Press, 1990).

Barna, George, **A Step-by-Step Guide to Church Marketing** (Ventura: Regal Press, 1992).

Callahan, Kennon L., **Twelve Keys to an Effective Church** (San Francisco: Harper, 1983).

Hacker, Andrew, **Two Nations: Blacks and White, Separate, Hostile, Unequal** (New York: Ballantine, 1992).

Kraft, Charles, **Christianity in Culture** (Maryknoll, NY: Orbis, 1979).

Miller, Herb, **How to Build a Magnetic Church** (Nashville: Abingdon, 1987).

Miller, Herb, **The Vital Congregation** (Nashville: Abingdon, 1990).

Naisbitt, John and Patricia Aburdene, **Megatrends 2000** (New York: William Morrow, 1990).

Sample, Tex, **U.S. Lifestyles and Mainline Religion** (Louisville: Westminster, 1990).

Schaller, Lyle, **It's a Different World** (Nashville, Abingdon, 1987).

Schaller, Lyle, **Strategies for Change** (Nashville, Abingdon, 1993).

Toffler, Alvin, **Powershift** (New York: Bantam, 1990).